emptiness
asian poems 1998–2012

Emptiness: Asian Poems 1998–2012 gathers together for the first time work John Mateer has written and on occasion published in South-East and North Asia. From the teeming cities of Singapore, Tokyo and Beijing to the quiet of a Malaccan street, a Honshu mountain or a Malay cemetery in Cape Town, Mateer journeys out into the unknown world and deep into the mind. His poems are patient investigations of language, selfhood and history. In the midst of an impressive oeuvre, *Emptiness* in particular complements and counterpoints its companion volume *The West: Australian Poems 1989–2009* and reveals the other side of life on our, eastern half of the globe.

First published 2014 by
FREMANTLE PRESS
25 Quarry Street, Fremantle 6160
(PO Box 158, North Fremantle 6159)
Western Australia
www.fremantlepress.com.au

Consultant editor Georgia Richter
Cover design Ally Crimp
Cover photograph detail from sculpture Everyone No. 177 by Rodney Glick
(Collection of Chris and Mary Hill)
Printed by Lightning Source, Victoria

National Library of Australia
Cataloguing-in-Publication entry

Mateer, John, 1971–, author
Emptiness: Asian poems 1998–2012 / John Mateer
Poetry
ISBN 9781922089625

A821.3

Government of **Western Australia**
Department of **Culture and the Arts**   lotterywest   Australian Government   Australia Council for the Arts

Fremantle Press is supported by the State Government through the
Department of Culture and the Arts.

Publication of this title was assisted by the Commonwealth Government
through the Australia Council, its arts funding and advisory body.

emptiness

asian poems 1998–2012

john mateer

FREMANTLE PRESS

ABOUT THE AUTHOR

John Mateer has published books of poems in Australia, Austria, Portugal and the UK, and smaller collections in South Africa, Indonesia, Japan and Macau. *World Literature Today* has called him "the most recent reincarnation of the international poet". He has won the Victorian Premier's prize for poetry and is a recipient of the Centenary Medal for his contribution to Australian literature. In Asia, he has been invited to read his work at Singapore's Wordfeast, at the Ubud and Galle writers festivals and at Tokyo's Festival of International Poetry. His latest books published in Australia are *The West: Australian Poems 1989–2009*, *Southern Barbarians* and *Unbelievers, or 'The Moor'*. Forthcoming are volumes translated into several European languages and Malay.

CONTENTS

11 MISTER! MISTER! MISTER!

13 TWO IMAGES

14 LOOKING AT A BOOK

15 THAT VOICE

16 BE CAREFUL,

17 AMOK: THE IMAGE

18 NO WOMAN ...

20 TRANSLATED MAN

21 THE MONKEY-SELLER'S STALL

22 THE ROCK

23 THIS PATH

25 TAKBIRAN

26 "BEFORE THE KA'ABAH"

27 ALLEYS

28 KRATON

29 RAIN

30 ANOTHER DREAM

31 CREMATION, BALI

33 MU NO BASHO

35 DEAD LEAVES OF TOKYO

36 INDUSTRY: TWO KINDS

38 THE COCKATOO

39 A PORTRAIT OF THE FUTURE

40 OSORE-ZAN

41 THE ANCIENT CAPITAL OF IMAGES

46 AUTUMN IS EVERYWHERE

47 SAIGYO'S CHERRY TREE

48 ON SEEING KINKAKU-JI

49 UNDER THE TEMPLE

51 THE DEEPEST NORTH

54 CONTEMPLATING A MIGRAINE

55 SINGAPORE AND THE REAL

57 AN IMPOSSIBLY GOLDEN LION REPEATEDLY GLIMPSED

58 THE SENSATION OF THE BORDER

60 EMBLEMS

61 SINGAPORE AND THE REAL

62 LEGENDS

64 SOMEONE WHO FREQUENTLY DISAPPEARS

65 "DESIRE IS THE TWIN OF CHAOS ..."

66 THE TEMPLE

67 ONE NIGHT

68 SLOWNESS, VIEWED FROM A BEACH ON SENTOSA

69 HAUNTINGS

71 INSTEAD OF A PANTUN

73 DARK BOOK

75 HAKUSHI

76 THIS DARK BOOK

77 TWO DREAMS

78 THE ABSTRACT

79 THE POET GLIMPSES HIS SOUL

80 AS IF TO MYSELF

81 DIGRESSION

82 'GHOST'

83 THE DREAM OF THE INAUDIABLE

84 THE POEM AS COMPETITION

85 AZURE NOISE

86 *PORTRAIT VON* _____

87 TREES

88 (INSCRIPTION)

89 THE ORIENTALIST

91 THE HIKAYAT ABDULLAH

94 "TUAN GURU" OF CAPE TOWN

95 KRAMAT

97 MIRROR

99 AT THE EMBASSY

100 MEETING A CHINESE POET

101 THE VASE

102 STELES

103 THE EMPEROR

104 RUIN: AN ESSAY

105 LILY

106 MORNINGS

107 "ICH BIN CHINESE"

108 IN THE MUSEUM

109 "CHEMIN DE L'ÂME"

110 LESSON ON ALLUSION

111 YINYUAN LONGQI *AKA* INGEN RYUKI

112 THE COUPLE

113 EXILE

114 GHOST WEDDING

116 AMONG THE MUSLIMS

117 THE POET

118 THE DREAMS

120 TO SEGALEN

121 THE KISS

122 THE DEMON

123 THAT POEM

124 LANDSCAPIST

127 ACKNOWLEDGEMENTS

"What are the most difficult things to paint?"
"Dogs and horses."
"And what are the easiest?"
"Ghosts."

– Han Fei, 234 BC

MISTER! MISTER! MISTER!

Your mouth is your tiger.

– Malay proverb

TWO IMAGES

The Jamu Pedlar

Every evening that tukang jamu passes my window
on her creaking bike. Under her bamboo hat, blouse
and black trousers her movements are rhythmic and slow,
like a Tibetan monk performing the mudras. Every evening
she clicks out her bike-stand to wait across the street
for her sole client, the exhausted man in torn clothes
from the scrapyard next door. Every evening he buys a glass,
gulping it down quickly. She speaks to him, but appears
wordless, silent. To the accompaniment of clinking bottles
and a glugging throat she is the ancient image of Grace.

The Dream

She has full, soft lips and is beautiful.
How he knows she is beautiful who can say?
She may be the image of the Malay bride on the travel guide's cover.
But she is faceless, not frightening,
and her bones curve with devotional time.
He is kissing her. They are naked. Then she is singing
in the only African language he can understand.
Her voice is a young woman desiring a child.
She is singing the lullaby or nursery rhyme with an elusive melody
that he has heard before, years ago, in another dream.
The echoing of her song could undo him if allowed to,
but before he can summon a word they are inaudible again.

LOOKING AT A BOOK

The pembantu, being illiterate,
holds the book awkwardly
– *It's a strange thing.*

She is tilting the book, like a mirror
or a large, disembodied ear.

She and her employer, the foreign poet,
across inarticulable space,
are studying the darkening time of photographs.

Together, the pembantu and the poet
are speaking the rare language of amazement.

THAT VOICE

       Is the voice that calls out
Mister! Mister! Mister!

       (a memory)

separate from the images of the beggar
       with withered legs whose arm reaches through the grille,

who grabs and grabs
at me across the space of

Mind?

BE CAREFUL,

be mindful if you wake someone here:
their soul could be away, wandering,

and mightn't return if you suddenly wake them
and they'd be left alone, insane, homeless.

Then you'd have to feed them as ghosts,
leaving bowls at intersections or outside your doors,

and they'd haunt you like an heredity disease
or the criminality of the invisible.

And then you'd have to attend to their graves
wherever you'd find yourself at rest,

and time's calm opposite would silence you with the vertigo
of all words returning, falling back into their mouths.

And your Self, in the senseless universe,
would be nothing but a photographic flaring.

Even though the sleeping may have been reincarnated already,
be careful: *Their worst nightmare is to be startled awake forever.*

AMOK: THE IMAGE

After the cloudburst, those leaves, glistening, sharpened,
are celestial machetes vividly mutilating space.

NO WOMAN ...

A photon ricochets through the wilderness of her skull.

Woman as cancer.

Her breath on any face is carbon monoxide.

Her flesh, haunting the world like a pornstar's,

is space.

~

> *Matahari, spy, sun, eye of the day who looks within!*

You aren't a surrogate mother,
Avalokitesvara's arms,
nor this Ramadan moon slicing off my fist.

You are the unknown body giving birth,
the ear agreeable in silence,
that darkness staring straight through us ...

~

Under his alien Caucasian skin,
her narcotic scent.

The pribumi woman yells at him,
I love you,

meaning: *You do not understand.*

~

The laugh following is an imploding star.

TRANSLATED MAN

To hear myself think in this noisy city I plug my ears.
Even the minarets are sirens and the daylight a thieving.
Here female eyes shout volumes at me.
Beside what was my soul, wordless men pedal their gliding becaks.
Through a phrasebook I stutter, bargain for space, mask disbelief.
Momentarily recognizing myself as the Marlboro man,
I return to the invisible.

> *In mimed song my lover's remembered voice taunts me.*
> *Her dancing body is the universe; its axis always a zero.*

In the desperate theatre of speech I dream ok.
Under the polychrome statuary of Kali's temple in Kampung Keling,
I fade out ok.
The translated man I am is becoming numerical: *zero, ok.*

THE MONKEY-SELLER'S STALL

The monkeys in the TV-sized cage at the roadside
have the faces of old men confronting death.
Under their black velvet fur, a pale immanence.

They stare at me with a terrible awe.
I am huge, monstrous, while they are splitting
like cells, like the infinity of mirror images.

Behind my skin there are clouds of smoke,
underground fires and this smothered city.

Through the mirror, I am watching the monkey-seller stalking.
I am watching one monkey in the seizure of screaming,
his voice an emptying.

In his agate-black eyes I am immediate and loss.

THE ROCK

The volcanic rock on my desk performs solidly.
I identify its presence.
It returns me to this room, this desk, this body.
I observe the rock. It is an eye heavy with silence.
It is an ear consuming space.
It is a memory of a clear day on the island of Samosir.
It is returning me to this room, this desk, my body.
Like Uluru, it confounds the astral, stating,
You do not know what it is you are like.
Personality, igneous rock and oblivion are the same.

THIS PATH

Anyone can walk this path where the eyes have no moon.
Who is to say there's ground under your feet,
except the odd brick crawling like a knocked-over animal?

     There's no light here only a dim sky hovering over the roofs.

Of the mouth that opens allowing the blackness in
– or the blackness out – your mind can only conjure
a vague angel.

~

Step carefully – there is a watery scattering of glass before you.

~

Have you never seen a mother sell an ulos for nothing?

Don't you understand that without a moon you, too, are ghostly?

~

Now, in the blackout, free of your silence,
you have turned onto a main street
and are starting to understand that there have been other ways...

     No, there is no music, few sounds.

Though the sudakos prowl like illuminated cages,
all the people are hushed, calm.

Candles and lanterns are glowing in the warungs.

In the alcoves of restaurants and stark doorless shops
every shadow is as precious as Coke crates or the shrines of ancestors.

~

In a moment of pure blackness,
as this city narrows to an alley,
all around you, in gutters, ditches, potholes, the rainwater
is now being struck

like a huge bell

~

and you are waking:

TAKBIRAN

There is a night when all radios transmit like minarets,
when the chanting of engines and firecrackers
is as comprehensive as the space in any loved room.

It's the night when windows tremble like the walls of Jericho,
when unbelievers acquiesce to the silence of their wide-screen TVs.

That night is stalked by a fasting moon and its thirsty day,
and with vibrato and reverb is everywhere breeding voices
like engineered wheat or a mirage in an Arabian desert.

That night is pursued by the single-eyed sun who squints
at the field of newspapers where families have knelt,
and squints again at them on scooters speeding to their ancestors.

On that night all is awake to the sound of the one Name.

"BEFORE THE KA'ABAH"

– after Sutardji Calzoum Bachri

That black meteorite,
outside metaphor:

Paradise …

ALLEYS

The Eye

Could say 'His', meaninglessly.

What matters is the convex, dark,
perfectly round eye, beneficent
only in that we are unreflected.

Around, aswirl, pixellations
of tiny feathers silver-edged
by morning.

Remind us, caged bird,
of someone other than Allah!

The Hand

It. Evokes hidden alleys
wherein polluted stars should be,

toothy mouths peopling
this walk's depthlessness.

Her's, illicit, is the warmth
of that congenial hand,

that moonlit, golden palm
and that – *imagined* – slap.

KRATON

Between the two bunyan trees
in the Kraton Square
a rumour could pass, ghostly,

a man, blindfolded,
walking backwards. *But which square?*
Don't you know there are two?

One of that quartet of trees
shattered the night the Sultan died.
A heart attack is never a murmur.

"Yet a rumour can be a coronary, Blind Man,"
said three of the trees, simultaneously.

RAIN

The rain, body temperature and linear, unlike a maternal phantasm,
varnishes the yard's banana leaves, atomizes the blurry streetlamps,
infiltrating minds as a surging brown equatorial river.

The river, twisting between decaying buildings and verdant wasteland,
is metallic with topsoil, incandescent as lava, blinding,
like the crackling of electricity and bone under my pale skin.

ANOTHER DREAM

You see yourself among the masses of pilgrims
gathered before dawn at Borobudur.

There in the crowd of worshippers
bearing the starlight of candles,

you are slowly ascending the steep igneous stairs
to circumambulate the stupa.

You are seeing your face, clearly,
among the many, as they gradually coil

around the monument
like the atoms of a holy, luminous snake.

CREMATION, BALI

(With the whoop of the mourners on the field,
under the marquee and the shaded dais,
the deceased man's daughter, grief-seized, collapsed,
weeping, is in the arms of a quick man,
removed lest the father's spirit remain here
wondering about her. The catafalque of wood and golden silk
collapsed in the long, tearing flames;
the white bull sarcophagus and bundled corpse fallen
into a timber mess so the cremators had to step forward,
practical as sailors, technicians of an ecstasy, with their long-tubed
blowtorches working at how matter resists combustion,
at how abandonment must be forced. In that fire I see the corpse
of my father, and of those 'comrades' bound in tyres and torched,
hated, during our wartime. Around me the villagers dressed in white,
no longer joking or greeting as they had in the temple,
watch on. Some eat fruit, drink bottled water,
or are making small offerings. Others, watching and quiet,
attend to their memories, outside of what grief
can grasp or sight hold as a glimpse.
Until the blackened, blowtorched parcel, shrunken, crumbles.
Even the skull, a smear of ashes
and flakes on the lightly damaged ground
over which individual hands will point out
what the large bamboo tweezers should find: grey shards
to be left, out-of-doors overnight, unattended,
for tomorrow's ceremony and their deliverance
in the nearby sea.)

MU NO BASHO

because there is no answer but emptiness

– Tamura Ryuichi

DEAD LEAVES OF TOKYO

Whether collected from the gardens of museums or temples
fallen leaves are an undoing of substance,
a subtle melancholia, an almost unheard-of music.

Bell-solid and a whispering, little deaths and the Chinese
                                        whimperings of memory,
those leaves under intense light on a city desk, observed
by a miniaturist's eye or a composer's ear, prove existence

as in the mind they are perpetuated in aquarelle,
each life-size on a page large and white and void.

        A chronicle, a diary?

The poet's mouth opens slowly, releasing the leaves and the wind
that these words are.

INDUSTRY: TWO KINDS

In a Public Park

Hammering. Dull hammering on a weekday morning.
The sound of early industry in Ueno Park.

The tourists ignore them, the employed have their own destinations,
while they, the homuresu, are already hard at work
pounding with mallets or half-bricks their store of recyclable cans.

A post-industrial metalwork, an unforging that begins with being
                                                                placeless,
with life under a blue tarpaulin on public land that was once a battlefield,
that begins with the civilization of the hammer upraised,
with each falling blow of that Iron Age tool, that icon of the proletariat,
that ends and begins mechanically in the morning light
here under a leafless cherry tree where a surplus

– an airy paragon of strength, the aluminium can –

is being repeatedly battered down, hammered flat
in hopes it will become a coin, a unit of exchange, a simple fact.

In the Pleasure Quarter

Being foreign is the democracy that allows the Nigerian,
in all the accoutrements of a gangsta, to address me as brother

and offer a special discount to a nice place where the girls are all foreign
– Russian, Brazilian, Australian – and all speak English.

We are, perversely, brothers: of the same continent,
slave and master, ear and mouth,

in the weird dialectic of Shinjuku, this thoroughfare
where crowds blur into clouds.

    What tradewinds brought him here? and those girls? and me?

Our common tongue is illusory, necessary, a kind of coin
minted by being stamped on.

THE COCKATOO

Off-white, the colour of one of those tapeworms in the Museum of
                                                          Parasites,
this spectre, this cockatoo, sulphur-crested and comatose.

I almost gassho to him in comradery –

he who like the sky glimpsed in a scooter's upturned mirror
is a respite from the harsh streetscape, an aperture.

I don't: this is a fluorescent-bright pet shop,

the kittens and puppies are sleepless in their hot perspex apartments,
the trendy customers – all couples – are mulling over *which one* to adopt

and the loud insistent throbbing could be a coronary intimation
of the legendary tattooed men: THE OWNERS.

The only stillness is this cockatoo, beak deep in the ruffle of his wing,
his sulphur crest fanned-in like the eyelashes of a dreaming girl.

A PORTRAIT OF THE FUTURE
–14 October 2002

Not even wincing, she is dripping scarlet wax onto her tongue now.
Before, she'd been bound, her flesh bundled by the rope,
her eyes erased by the white virginal cloth.

On TV in my modern hotel room I am watching her
as I will watch footage from the new war, hesitating –

     Is she an exorcist,
or a martyr offering herself to salarymen and bondage masters
as a mother gives of herself to her children?

Or is she, in her corporal solitude, a butoh dancer
spasmodic in the atomic cloud of the everyday,
a witness – inarticulate – to the new psyche?

Now she is pixilated, censored, blocks of fleshtone
     – where her torturer is touching her –
becoming abstraction, totalized, the dissolving face

that in my dark mind after I've switched the TV off is radiant.
Not an afterimage – a ghostly portrait of our future.

OSORE-ZAN

Nearing the edge of the crater lake, that dead mirror,
        I observed my existence here, that in this no-man's-land,
this Bardo, on this, another mountain, I was seeking my lost.

        Among the thrown coins,
the statues of Jizo shabby in stillborn children's clothes,
among their pink plastic windmills and incomplete stupas
of loose gritty stones,

I was watching my reflection drifting over the jaundiced ground,
over its steaming, burping holes,
ghosting through the blank banners of sulphurous smoke.

This is what the Earth has vomited up in unwelcome:
a foretaste of Hell.

Yet in the pacifying mirror that I am,
        all this is merely the melted ruin of my mother's house,
my father's ashes cast to the wind on an African mountain
in his family's absence, the wasteland of my childhood –
factories, pasty yellow tailings dams and, the only mountains I knew,
grassed-over minedumps.

What I am seeing is Hell, nothing other than waste
and its gesture: abandonment.

THE ANCIENT CAPITAL OF IMAGES

Sanjo-dori

His shop is deep and dim, like the cavity left in the face
after an eye has been removed. Less a shop than a stall
or a rummage sale opened out onto the street,
except that this man is a merchant of pornography and nobody is buying.

At the back, watching through the wooden window frame,
he's stooped, cross-legged on the tatami
with the orange glow of the gas heater menacing behind him.

    He has that sickness, those eyes.

    Smells like the den of a dying thing.

    What is that pain? an image?

The magazines: women in kimonos, bound with rope, tethered to beds
                                        or chairs,
their long hair occult, bewitchingly uncurling,
their nude faces transported, distant,
their inaudible, contorted spirits being

    (the Ancient Capital during one of its fires,
a world floating on the canals and rivers
that pull our images away)

Hanamikoji-dori

Those words have been said so many times by her voice
that she doesn't hear them. A modern philosopher thought Nothingness
was the lining of a kimono; but what of her dress?
an anorak that reaches down to her stilettos, can't keep out the cold.
Isn't Nothingness the body?

What she offers on this back street after the freezing hostesses
have bade their clients farewell is a skin-deep kindness.

I like her face.

Emotional pain can be washed from the body.

How?

It might take many lifetimes.

I like her face. I imagine her naked, her skin against mine, warming.
The fur of two animals.

And her mind would be elsewhere, away from the false,
not Nothingness, not a place of meeting,
and this city would be

(*the Ancient Capital during one of its fires,
a world floating on the canals and rivers
that pull our images away*)

Nanzen-ji

The crouching amateur photographers, with that enthusiasm,
have set up their cameras, telescopic lenses tilted skyward targeting
the small maple, that one branch overhanging
the canal of white noise that's streaming down from the mountain.

Its leaves are a vermilion incandescence,
blood vessels in a blushing, transparent face.

The colour of the momentary,
that's what they're fixing out there in the blinding world.

Could you do that?

Behind my eyes,
  a geisha in the crowd at the Saturday night traffic lights,
her kimono a golden brocade landscape, her skin a primal white.

  The sexual is a binding, a garden behind thick stone walls.

  And also behind my eyelids,
kidnapped by the visible – a strobe light's staccato,
the ochre-white Aboriginal man
dancing,
  stamping in the talc dust.

  You are nearing the Place of Nothingness,

  (the Ancient Capital during one of its fires,
a world floating on the canals and rivers
that pull our images away)

GO FURTHER –

Shijo-dori

The crouching amateur photographers, with that enthusiasm,
have set up their cameras, telescopic lenses tilted skyward targeting
the small maple, that one branch overhanging
the canal of white noise that's streaming down from the mountain.

Its leaves are a vermilion incandescence,
blood vessels in a blushing, transparent face.

The colour of the momentary,
that's what they're fixing out there in the blinding world.

Would you dare do that?

Behind my eyes,
        a geisha in the crowd at the Saturday night traffic lights,
her kimono a golden brocade landscape, her skin a primal white.

The sexual is a binding, the garden behind ancient stone walls,

a place of emptiness,

(the Ancient Capital during one of its fires,
a world floating on the canals and rivers
that pull our images away)

Ponto-cho

She's refilling my glass with Jinro while the proprietor is mashing
the raw egg and spicy sauce into the rice for me. Outside
the neon signs are looking for their reflections on the sides of polished taxis
and the unlit shrine for a beheaded family withdraws from street-side

conversation.

She's talking to me: "Kampai!" The quiet proprietor returns my
bowl. She's saying: "This is her way: from Korea ..."

They nod, would say other things.

The two men at the counter speak better English.

An everyday thing, how to eat your food.

They would have said –

With the metal chopsticks, with restful deliberation,
I eat as though

(the Ancient Capital during one of its fires,
a world floating on the canals and rivers
that pull our images away)

AUTUMN IS EVERYWHERE

                              Even in an explosion
if you have the right shutter speed: the shards of rock

– projectiles – will become fluttering leaves decorating an icy wind.
Autumn is everywhere. Autumn is your skin flaking,

those shards becoming boulders offered to the eye
of an electron microscope, becoming food for dust mites,

becoming the conundrum of The Instant:
How can moments, things, have an independent existence?

Yet, if found among the scattered remains of an explosion,
the shards of my canines and molars will prove my existence.

Everywhere I look the avenues of trees are exploding in slow motion.

SAIGYO'S CHERRY TREE

The spirit of Saigyo's cherry tree is waiting there for me in my dream.
An old man, armoured in a business suit, his face a Shiwajo mask,
he asks me what I meant by writing – *The colour of the momentary,*
that's what they're photographing out there in the blinding world.
Momentarily I see the four hundred other cherry trees alive with
blossoming,
then see myself as a joyful young husband on his wedding day,
those blossoms bright confetti tossed on a warm wind.
The colour of the momentary in a blinding world?
I don't know how to reply to the spirit of a tree.
Actually he's the spirit of the blossoms.
That's what they're photographing out there in the blinding world!
the colour of the momentary! he shouts,
then disappears in a blinding whiteness.
And I'm waking to remember that one hibakusha,
in a letter to his wife's spirit, evoked their fateful moment
as an enormous blue-white flash,
as when a photographer lights a dish of magnesium.

ON SEEING KINKAKU-JI

Upside down on your retina, on the nerves deep in the black box
                                                    of your skull,
the Pavilion, radiant, wobbling, gently righting itself,
like a tethered boat after being disturbed by a passing wave.

On the pond there are two Golden Pavilions: the Real and its
                                                    reflection.

Unlike Mishima's antihero, you don't wonder whether beauty is
                                            the burning pavilion
or its surrounding void.

        Your body, obscure, sees itself – wrapped in gold leaf, an eyeball –
and in that impulse, the desire to remember, to photograph,
you notice that on the apex of the roof
of this treasure once torched by a monk,

there stands, arched and alarmed, an airy, comic phoenix.

UNDER THE TEMPLE

Sentience – mine – reduced to my right hand,
its fore- and middle-finger dragging along the timberwork.
Feelers. A consciousness shrunk to wisps.

> *No eye ear nose tongue body mind*
> *No colour sound scent taste touch thought*

Darkness. What we are withdrawn from us.
Impossible, you believe, in this millennium
burning like a neon mansion.

> *No eye ear nose tongue body mind*
> *No colour sound scent taste touch thought*

Above or below, in front or behind,
merely notions whispered by the crystals of our inner ear,
our spirit-level. Brilliant metaphors.

> *No eye ear nose tongue body mind*
> *No colour sound scent taste touch thought*

What I am under the thick floors of Zenko-ji,
after twice turning in this blacked-out passage,
this invisible, acoustically dead cathedral –

> *No eye ear nose tongue body mind*
> *No colour sound scent taste touch thought*

are those memories, those imaginings.

No eye ear nose tongue body mind
No colour sound scent taste touch thought
No seeing and so on to …

The blindness is a golden wilderness.

THE DEEPEST NORTH

Of the Northern Peoples

Gold teeth rock-logical in his mouth, his face
a wall of crumpled paper smoothed out into smiles.
He stops chuckling, stares at me,
his eyes animal, courageous in their simple darkness,
and I am an horizon.

Of a people used to staring out into the white, into blindness,
he could be a prehistoric explorer hurtling on a sled,
skidding, bouncing across the blue icefloe,
his breath a frosty pennant, his laugh wild as Creation.

Fleetingly he's Hone, a roshi, a connoisseur of raw flesh, wind.
Then he's Yamamba, the Mountain Crone, my dying self
wordlessly screaming:

On Asahi-dake

The rock is large enough to block the wind if I crouch down
like a primitive man inventing shelter. I do.

And from here on Asahi-dake my view is of the distant mountain range
and a nearby gravel slope where, with streaming smoke,
the Earth is pouring into the grey sky and howling endlessly
jet-engine harsh through the holes of its volcanic vents, its exhausts.

Whole industrial cities could be buried here under the rubble
right up to the tips of their smokestacks.

Why do mountains always miniaturize the human,
reduce us to an imagining?

I wait there until the mist descends,
then wander the stony paths until I am lost in the whiteness.

Encountering a Bear

Facing the Sea of Okhotsk, to my right the mouth of the invisible
Iwaobetsu River,

to my left the stretch of beach, not grey in this autumn twilight, dim,
another density of dark, though not the solid black of the volcanic cliffs.

Dull waves forming and re-forming the intermittent shore –

Words, phonemes, breaking down, sizzling.

Behind, high up on the cliff road, amber stars flashing: road-safety beacons.

Then on the beach some distance off, a large rock becomes two rocks,
single, then twinned, to and fro, flickering in my vision, larger, approaching.

There's not a sound, only the impossibly black form nearing me fast
as a bear.

There's no sound, nor do I know I'm running, flying over the lumpy sand,
the stones, the thick grass …

I am horned, a stag fleeing, prey-mute.

CONTEMPLATING A MIGRAINE

Words, there are for this, but the *thing* – a distant flaring
under the crust of my skin, deep inside its shifting homeliness.

Pain: the purest life. I could start to pray …

Through the window, as compensation, the rain gently gives me
the garden,
its mossy rocks, its green benevolence, the garden that drops away

into the soaring cedar forest suggestive of the opposite of whatever
this pain is.

I would say, *a kind of mountain.*

But maybe I am the mountain,
and the pain, hidden in cloud, is a foreboding shrine, unvisited.

SINGAPORE AND THE REAL

... there is no future in nostalgia.

– Arthur Yap

AN IMPOSSIBLY GOLDEN LION REPEATEDLY GLIMPSED

As if solidity underwrites everything we touch, this land reclaimed
from the flat gunmetal sheen of the Singapore Straits

is under my feet as innocent beach sand imported from a rasping aftermath.
Meanwhile, around an island in Riau's elsewhere,

the tide is rising, waves arriving, finally, at a rudimentary house door
– an impossibly golden lion repeatedly glimpsed, unnamed.

The footprints of my silence are inventing this elsewhere
and my sight recalling the freighters and cargo-ships queued up out there
                                                                last night,

their pinprick profiles alternate coastlines
shaped by the curious hands of the recently blind.

The coconut palms, the trees alert with nocturnal green and the families
whose Friday night camp-out was another elsewhere are now definite
                                                                memories,

as are the Special Operations trainees in their sweat-soaked overalls,
their yellow numbers – not names – shouted after them
                                all along the length of East Coast Park,

as is the tiny feral cat who after midnight prowls the beach resort,
a white blur, a lynx, that beast whose waves of low, slow howling
                                are arriving, finally, at my villa's open door.

THE SENSATION OF THE BORDER
– for Musa

In the shade cast by the tall palm tree beside him
my ex-student's face has the momentary flatness of an obscured photo.

While behind, across the Causeway
that divides the economy of today from yesterday's,

across the land bridge that he once touched
from a canoe after a week-long circumnavigation

of his island-country, Malaysia is shining office towers,
condos, paradisial shopping and a deception.

~

In our casual senses
    the circling of a stupa
is not commerce,

    but is, like a kindly
gripping of a hand,
    an exponential happiness,

a Being-in-the-
    round that can reclaim
from the obscure, insistent

    flatness of a photo
a new friend's face,
    distant, persistent,

smiling:

EMBLEMS

Daydreaming that orchid, looking
at what I can never see:

that Technicolor cocktail splashed
up against my crude face,

a gilded, spangled
lizard rising again suddenly

frilled out –

SINGAPORE AND THE REAL

That something exists doesn't necessarily mean that it's real.
That person gliding down the narrow monochrome passage of a hotel
                                                    in China Town
you are watching on the CCTV monitor needn't be me,
nor does the gaze of a young woman that lingers too long on my face
in the Lunar New Year's Eve crowd necessarily imply a future kiss.
That dusk invokes in Little India a neon yellow trident on a dim temple,
the scarlet moons of those lanterns over Desker Street's conspicuously
                                                    unattended doors
as well as those Golden Arches at the corner,
and on other streets the litter in the gutters, the mangos in boxes,
the baroque sweep of labourers' hands sopping up curry with naan,
and the poet who admires the tango-closeness
of two cars edging around one another in a lane, needn't mean
that previous empires existed nor that we will see ourselves
in tomorrow morning's bathroom mirror. *Well,* you might muse,
while watching me on the monitor in your hidden office,
I am God and he my clay –
Should I send him past the spruikers outside the restaurants and bars
                                                    at Boat Quay?
Or should I force his mouth open with a karaoke microphone in a Katong dive?
Or bang the sky with fireworks that he won't see
except as trailing tinsel on the vast glass skyscrapers?
And as those thoughts gather, this shrinking island, this tropical city-state
– as much as your Poet – is something that is sung into being and exists,
though that doesn't mean that it's real, necessarily.

LEGENDS

A few years later,
trying to evoke
in mind
that photograph
seen at Du Fu's
house in Chengdu,
which showed
the visiting Lee Kwan
Yew, I can't
remember if Mao
was there
beside him,
though I am sure
the plaque
had him nameless,
as simply 'President
of Singapore',
whether in Mandarin,
too, I'm not sure,
and I was reminded
of the poet,
gay, practitioner
of capoeira,
who had to remove
a verbal image
of that president
riding a paper tiger
so his poem
could appear
in the newspaper.

He also collaborated
on a shadowy
play about
the legend,
Annabel Chong
the Lion City's Gangbang
Queen, she,
whom I can remember
clearly in the documentary
on her life,
ended up
alone in a ghetto
apartment in LA,
cheated by the pornographers
and shouting her name
repeatedly into the phone,
asking: "Don't
you know who
I am?"

SOMEONE WHO FREQUENTLY DISAPPEARS

–for Zai Kuning

As if he wasn't waiting for me he was, on Armenian Street
in the kopitiam, rising from a circle of familiars,
gliding towards me like the Orang Laut
for whom he once waited on a beach in Riau year-long
until that one dawn. Extending his hand, we greet like Malays
                                        everywhere;
he a nomad, I an exile, both of us friends in a poem by Rumi.
And we speak of histories before the city-state,
of Araki who sees women in bondage as yellow hybrid orchids
                                        splattered with red,
until we stroll through the steamy night to the bus stop
and I depart like a sea-gypsy, sailing high in the front window
                                        of the double-decker bus,
watching far below the rain-slicked streets parting like waves, darkly.

"DESIRE IS THE TWIN OF CHAOS ..."

Their tongues flickered
     like two birds locked in a taxi
as voices argued that
     desire is the twin of Chaos
and the unrequited is that gap
     palpable between every heartbeat.

Past signboards warning of lightning storms
     and deadly, tumbling coconuts,
the couple wandered whispering,
     while all along the shore the Straits
licked its
moonlit lips.

THE TEMPLE

Inside this Chinese box of a city, in this quiet temple,
this phantasmal palace as miniscule as Heaven,

I am beside the alms box, chained to a perch.
I am that ruffled sulphur-crested cockatoo,

this albino sage who, disconsolate, caws
in Portuguese:

Look for me over there.

ONE NIGHT

Out of a bhangra nightclub and its Bollywood writhing
– the Tamil drummer of mind, turbaned, arm raised still
in the zenith of a throb – you emerge
into an impossibly deserted Orchard
where the taxis are freeze-framed
and the road is slick and black
and steaming like new, hardening lava
and everyone is blurred by alcohol,
sweating with all the effort of world creation,
and the only – if that may be named – 'action'
are those ladyboy's eyes enervating every

    (YOU).

SLOWNESS, VIEWED FROM A BEACH ON SENTOSA

(like a whiter cloud hyperextended, or a glass of water
rotated by a patient, plural earth –
the barge I am watching from this ersatz tropical beach
is, in its paralleling the silvered horizon
of water warm-as-skin,)

(an anti-time, elasticating my senses,
so that its diesel, chugging,
and its daydreaming skipper, and its cargo of sand,
are as elemental as any harbour returned to,

any body known as your own)

HAUNTINGS

Story

His aunt, who had been having evil visions off and on for several months, had deteriorated so badly that the family had decided to consult a dukun. The dukun met my friend's aunt, and after a few failed attempts to find the cause, understood that it was not stemming directly from her nor from anything she had done. He believed an ancestor was angry. After investigating the family's genealogies, he had them make another appointment. He explained that that the ancestor had been angered because my friend's niece hadn't been married following the appropriate Malay rites. The aunt then spoke up, recalling that her daughter hadn't worn the correct kebaya and sarong. They had fought about that on the wedding day, her daughter telling her not to be so old-fashioned. The dukun wasn't surprised. "That is why the Devil is bothering your aunt. To correct this, her daughter must remarry in the presence of the ancestor. You must hold the wedding at the Kramat of Raden Mas, so She and the other spirits can see that you have found and corrected the error." They made the arrangements, not telling everyone in the family, only those directly involved. The dukun came to the kramat to conduct the ceremony. My friend, his sister and his mother were there. As soon as the rituals began, it became overcast. Then dogs started barking and howling. There was thunder, and then the rain began. At first everyone was only a bit afraid, concentrating on the dukun's chanting and on the stillness of the couple, only occasionally glancing at his aunt beside the couple being remarried. She was transfixed, staring blindly, her lips moving in silent prayer. Without saying anything, suddenly, my friend's sister arose and began to dance, with all the grace of a traditional

Javanese court dancer, perfectly, as if she were Keramat of Radin
Mas, this girl who had never had a dance lesson in her life, whose
hobby was indoor rockclimbing, and whose only visits to her
spiritual homeland had been to the messy city of Jakarta. As she
danced, they knew the Ancestors were there, and that the dukun
had been right. Just as suddenly as she had begun, she stopped
dancing, and the storm abated. Later, when they had told her
what had happened, she'd said she had no memory of that. My
friend had videoed it all, and said he could show me, were he not
afraid to copy the computer file. "My auntie is now much better,"
he assured me. He told me this story one evening to explain why
we hadn't been able to meet the last time I was in Singapore.

Hantu

In the centre of night, of a dream,
I woke, panicked, beside my lover,
as after an argument or before a scream,
and had in my wild, dizzy head
that local hill, bare and luminous green,
watchful as a hantu, unnamed, unseen.

INSTEAD OF A PANTUN

Outside your hotel in Malacca
you will hear the tiny howling

of a feral kitten filling the street
with the backwash and silence

that foretells a tsunami,
and on your mind's emptied beach

there will be a lynx seen elsewhere
and on your tongue

the Name for all that's hidden ...

DARK BOOK

Thine eyes not thine noise waked me.

– John Donne

HAKUSHI

What might be a brushstroke's inky black
is, in perpetuity, the trembling hand
lifting that brush into the BLANK –

THIS DARK BOOK
– on a photo album by Daido Moriyama

This dark book the size of a box of ashes
is one memorial after another, page after page
of stills, as if we could be cinematic,
as if sight were never an erasure, that metaphysical black.

Were we idols in the Hollywood we imagine, toned flesh
slicked silver or, better, shimmering with the golden applause
of days flashing past, page after page,
we would never have doubted the photographic,

never have hoped for the abandon of a poem.

TWO DREAMS

Nagano

In the chill that always precedes snowfall,
on that morning I would walk up the cobbled street to Zenko-ji,
where, after kneeling for hours, each painful knee a bright skull,
I would turn and turn in the blackness beneath the altar,
muttering a poem in anti-mantra, circling the stupa of ex-Self,
and dream that my father, gaunt in a red kimono,
having returned from world in which he was more present
than in life, smiled a foreign kindness
and handed me, a gift wrapped in gold leaf
– a wagashi eye – that I wanted to eat but didn't.

Kyoto

The first night I slept in the farmhouse,
under the thatch and dark timber, deep in the noiselessness,
I dreamed that in the next room, there on the Other Shore,
across the hearth's infernal pit, there where bright motes
dart nervously across an eye's lacquered brush,
a woman in a moth-white nightdress, her hair
flung forward over her face and dangling, was paused
like a dawn tree burdened with dew,
and I immediately knew that she was a warning:
a glistening tongue wriggling in a mute's mouth.

THE ABSTRACT

Here in the Museum of the Twenty-Six Martyrs of Japan
you will find a tiny Eighth Century Kannon,

an old Korean woman mossy with oxidation,
limbs looped out, visage pensive, attentive, a young mother's

as she watches over her newborn, still marvelling
at its penile flesh and unconscious godliness.

This was worshipped for hundreds of years
by the Hidden Christians of the Goto Islands

as the Virgin Mary, not as Kuan-yin
or Miao-shan or Avalokitesvara.

To you she is not even a statue,
more an imperfectly understood operating system,

a convolution of nerves
interrupted by the scalpel of an impatient God.

THE POET GLIMPSES HIS SOUL

Photograph by Araki

Rope knotted around her neck binds her to the bed
from opposite directions. Her kimono is wrenched open
and her breasts are small, paper-smooth under the incomprehensible,
emphatic kanji of her nipples. She is staring at you,
her eyes on you, each lens-cold, surgically discriminating,
focused on you like magnifying glasses sharpening the rays of
                                                    twin suns
to patiently ignite the trash heap of your Soul.

Crows of Shinjuku

Unsteady crows hopping from one bulging garbage bag
to another in the Shinjuku morning;
what was my Soul, its incomplete sentences,
its buccaneers, springing ashore, desperate to remember
where they inhumed the treasure.

AS IF TO MYSELF

Your eyes, dear Poet,
close your eyes, *this brothel
is the only world*, and see
that she is the bodhisattva;
open your eyes and say:

YOU ARE THE BODHISATTVA

DIGRESSION

Again the black Portuguese ships with their sails battened down
are gliding towards a gold-leaf shore; sans memories
of jagged iron seas or phosphorescent mermaids,
bringing the good news of gunpowder, porcelain and The Word.

On a splendid screen this was painted with the calm of an assured politics,
with the gentle humour of a sensei who restates his theme
with digressions:

> *Did you notice those dusky sailors high up in the rigging,*
> *clambering or perched or dangling, like trapeze artists?*
> *And you thought all black men were American!*

'GHOST'

Each of those synonyms
for the word 'ghost',
translated from a dream,
will be a glassy eye
witnessing the phantasm
that, in its stereoscopic presence,
will always be a gagged voice
murmuring entries
from the Thesaurus of Pain.

THE DREAM OF THE INAUDIBLE

"Don't worry, in this dream you won't have to speak."

"In this dream you will be The Excluded, beheaded."

"Your voice will be the shushing of a jugular fountain."

"In this dream not even I, The Invisible, will exist."

THE POEM AS COMPETITION

– for Keiji Minato

The translator and I were writing the same poems
in this dream:

Hurry! Hurry, before one of us wakes!

AZURE NOISE

Her hair: quick as a whip,
a fountain luminous
and truly blonde;
mouth: a deep, moist imploding.

      "Grip my throat and squeeze."

Anything other, every other
'thing' I can remember,

though she must have been only
the branches of a cherry tree,
blossoms shaken at a pessimistic wind.

"Squeeze my throat. Tighter."

Eyes: dilating.

      (Only silent fireflies rising
    from invisible shrubs,
    their erratic golden flickering,
    like specks of traffic seen
    from the Mito Tower):

her – unavoidable – *Voice*.

PORTRAIT VON _____

– after Furuya Seiichi

This poem will be written with a book of photographs
in mind, commemorating that picture of the young
art history student who would become the photographer's
wife, the mother of his son, she who would fling herself
from the window of their apartment, who, because
she had existed, would proliferate,
like all that can be said by The Unspoken.

TREES

The woman whose home had been erased by fire
dreamed that the avenue to her rebuilt house,
that phosphorescent shock of blossoming cherry trees,
had been uprooted –

    "I no longer interpret dreams."

(INSCRIPTION)

The ex-White poet reminiscing with the Dejima Tree spoke soundlessly.

THE ORIENTALIST

I noticed that his behaviour was almost like that of a small human being, save only that he lacked the power of speech.
– The Hikayat Abdullah

THE HIKAYAT ABDULLAH, or An Orientialist's Fable

– for Harry Aveling

Whenever Abdullah remembered the orang-utan
the Sultan of Samba had sent as a gift
to Raffles, with the slaves whom the Great Man always freed,
he would see that creature in hat and suit

sitting beside him – 'The Malay' – while he was scribing.
Once the orang-utan lifted the pen from his desk
and with two fingers held it as if to write,
only to calmly replace the small instrument,

having the good grace of animal restraint
and, perhaps, an intimation of the ruin that's possible
when words outlive one, speaking ghostly
as from somewhere inside a distant stranger.

Like the wisdom of not staring at a mirror
for too long, not marvelling at your existence,
thought Abdullah, the Translator and Autobiographer,
smiling ironically as he made note of that.

He wondered if that was what Raffles had seen
– Himself – when, on the island of Saint Helena, he visited
the exiled Napoleon, that Image of Conqueror.
Was our English Raffles an adequate mirror?

"A seeker? Like my orang-utan," he found himself writing,
"who, when his mate had passed away, pined
and starved himself, becoming a small ghost,
a few days later his presence almost optical error.

As a translator Abdullah hoped that he, too, had Fidelity.
When Mister Milne was astonished at all the Malay names
for spirits and ghosts, Abdullah enumerated
them further, saying that they should be captured

– *Inshallah!* – in a book so that they would cease to exist,
interfering, as they do, with the purer words
of Allah; Arabic no kin to Abdullah's
other tongues, no brother to Malay, Tamil or English,

nor to Hindi, Hakka or Cristao. We know angels
only speak Arabic, just as Archangel Gabriel
did into Mohammad's ear, then He to the Scribe, not Translator.
The Prophet knew there is neither Image nor Mirror

enough for the Great God of the Singular. Abdullah,
still writing, remembered how he had explained
the nature of an eclipse to his native friends:
"No, it is not Allah stepping in front of the moon!

Not, as Chinese think, the moon eaten by a dog!
Not as Hindus assume, swallowed by a snake!"
None of them would believe his Western account,
its abstractions, cryptic mathematics and magic.

Samsara is an even worse idea, Abdullah thought.
Life is not solely suffering. When his daughter died,
he and his wife could not cease their weeping.
One day, at her grave, he saw the little girl alive,

awaiting his embrace, and he rushed to her.
She disappeared. He then composed a poem for all deceased
children, reminding their parents that they would again be united
in Heaven. When every one of his possessions were burnt

on a Lunar New Year's Eve in Singapore,
the entire city – all the kampungs – trembling and molten,
streams of opium treading the streets, pouring
through screams, bubbling up as smoke, even then

and there he began composing a syair, a long poem
against amnesia. One mind is never memory enough.
He wrote that down, then thought, cheekily,
Not even Raffles' brain! Besides, that eccentric Englishman,

unbeknownst to our Abdullah, would nowhere
mention his Scribe and Teacher, nor the man's – typical of Malay
copyists – embellishments, nor his honest, returned stare
into the deep eyes of man or orang-utan to allay

grief. Whatever is seen is always those flames
goldleafing the World, that with Absence will chew through us
as the ship's fire did through all the Archipelago's manuscripts and books
in Raffles' possession on the homeward-bound steamer FAME.

That is the Vanishing. Yet there is also the perpetually heard.
Looking over his pages of Jawi script, Abdullah shook his head,
his tired eyes almost seeing other words – Arabic, Hindi, Tamil,
Roman – and, sleepy, he sensed that he himself might almost be

an orang-utan,

silent, in an Orientalist's fable.

"TUAN GURU" OF CAPE TOWN

When one is exiled from land and language,
as I was, and brought to another island,
a windy, rocky prison named after the seals there,
it is best not to hate. Better to cultivate a garden
or build a palace in one's heart. They call me "Tuan Guru",
I, Abdullah ibn Kadi Abdus Salaam, the Prince of Tidore
who sided with the English ... My garden is the sprawling
manuscript scribed in my cell, mouthed in Arabic,
every second line a mirror-image in Malay
or Bugis. In the Name of Allah, I wrote for us
to remember His Twenty Attributes. We understand this.
Christians never will. We twist their tongue, too. The word
for "prison" is ours. Not Dutch or Malay: *Balinese.*
A native of Paradise named that kind of hell!
In my book I included talismans, too. We need
pure words to save us from the echoing that is everywhere.
Each European voice threatens us in the marketplace.
All for cloves and other spices, those wars,
I reminded myself as in my cell I sat,
dedicated to copying our Holy Book. That is why
we built the Dorp Street Madrassah where I am now
Imam, and why I appointed Damon of Bugis to teach
Arabic to the children and illiterates. I, Iskander
Shah of the Cape! If, as our Rumi wrote, our souls
are indeed from elsewhere, and we are to speak forever
only our Kitchen-Dutch, fellow Exiles and Slaves,
my Brothers and Sisters, remember: *Never hate.*
Remember: *The Heavenly Palace, untranslated,*
is in your hearts.

KRAMAT

– for "the Friends"

"Cover your head with a cloth, hide your face.
You are a cave … "

See, there you are at the Malay Burial Ground
over the Mother City and the iron Atlantic, there
where the slave rebellion began. You are at the kramat
praying to someone believing him to be Tuan Guru.
He listens from the tomb next door,
smiles silently. Your desperation, Poet, paying homage
at the wrong grave! Meanwhile, near, in a shack
at the back of another's house – the tiny yard paradisal
with its lemon tree – Tatamkhulu, Friend, He of Five Names
and of Afrika, is awaiting you. Unlike you, Death
kept his appointment. You will again read Tata's
last letter – "Why do you not return to Azania,
help us rebuild this country?" – in an underground carpark
in Australia and you will weep: Sins of the Fathers!
There are those Patriarchs who accompany
you, as the translucent lion did Abn al-Farid
on his daily traverse between his home and Mecca,
to the Ka'abah, that great Imageless Mother.
Don't send out from this cave dreams of severing
detractors' tongues hoping to save your name! In this cave,
Poet, the lion is leading you through the blue mangroves of Singapura
to find Wak Ali Janggut stunned at Siti Maryam's kramat,
bulldozer stomping, aching at the bloodied tree.
Bearded Ali who in the oceanic underworld, drowning,
heard Her Voice and was luminous,
ascending through clouds of cinnamon seaweed.

She had saved him, her Little Brother. So he made a custodial vow.
Now the tree shatters like a window, a boy steps out
from the rubble. Did Bearded Ali weep? Abdullah the Translator,
did see djinns resisting the demolition of Melakka's fort.
Here, in your cave, you huddle with the other bereft,
and with Zai. His memorial to his Teacher a massive log
half-sutured with nails and metal tread. He declared
that was his Teacher's corpse, his spirit a vast, invisible tree.
All caves are a gaol cell and a blacked-out auditorium. Hear
now those friends just returned from Kashgar; hear Ali
the Memoirist laughing that another friend had penned the Persian word
for "far away" – PERTH – over the gateway of the city's mosque;
and Layli confiding that she sometimes feels the Friend is near,
that were He to ask her to accompany Him she would,
without question ... Now, Poet, you are remembering Mysterious
Ghassan, another poet, in Coimbra, in Café Santa Cruz, the hush
and reverb of vaulted ceiling, clinking wineglasses, his voice
raspy with cigarettes: "Tomorrow I return to the cave,
to Palestine ... " Here in the darkness your voice
is walking away. What holds you here, Poet?
A tree? Your tree is burning, a sun of embers
festering under its blackened skin.

"Don't lift your shroud yet!"

MIRROR

O you, will you not translate yourselves?
– Victor Segalen

AT THE EMBASSY

Being diplomatic,
speaking both tongues,
they are launching
a book, CITIZENS,
like a ghost-ship.

MEETING A CHINESE POET

You are one of the delegation sent to meet the poet. At the railway station, standing in the shade, you stare north into the glare. The day is peaceful, one of those filled with continental solitude. Next to you along the platform there are dwarfs, silent and motionless. You are on the verge of remarking on this when, soundless, the train arrives, its doors sighing open. The poet in cheap clothes steps out, his face that of a man who has been released from prison only to find no-one awaiting him at the gate.

THE VASE

Evoked by the slave's
voice, the vase
is unmade
by the master.

The vase, vocal
labour, is the slave's
site of crazed
manufacture.

To collect her tears
the slave must shatter
the vase, remake
everyone's voice;

to recollect tears
she must make,
of everyone's voice,
a shadow vase.

STELES

The Forest of Steles in memory
is the razed house of the Poem,
gravestones facedown on the earth
like Segalen's Stele of the Middle,
speaking to God's inner ear
as if He could allow a Kingdom
other than the Han, his own.
The steles in the basement
of the National Gallery of Australia,
where Papuan artefacts have been forgotten,
were jungles of utterance clear-felled,
imitative Tang songs like stone animals
chasing one another along a frieze
while frozen. The Forest's guardian,
a Cassandra, with a pen dipped
in water, wrote:

I AM THE MOMENT.

His script could be another memorial
to Empress Wu's Wordless Stele,
its uninscribed, expectant panegyric.
Some joke that the tabula rasa
reads:

Perpetual fear.

THE EMPEROR

There is, in the plush womb of the Macau casino,
your Emperor of Dead Languages, whispering persistently

into the ear of a Slavic lady-of-the-night. In Korean?
Those women learn the lingo first; subtle adventurers

of the Hidden. Always internationalists, they understand
that a North Korean dictator's son, as much as a sinophilic French poet

has visions in which He Who Decrees

    will have spoken,

and He Whose Words Are Engraved In Stone is always

godly mute.

RUIN: AN ESSAY

This vast country's first and most important modern ruin,
claims the art-historian in his book on The Contemporary,
was the Place of Perfect Brightness, pillaged
by French and Dutch troops, and also Gordon of Khartoum.
(Elsewhere I've read Gordon confess to his mother:
"It was demoralizing work for an army. Everybody was wild
for plunder.") One hundred and twenty-one years later
an unofficial poetry reading was photographed there.
In the picture, faces obscured to protect their identities,
those youths are a cabal, occultists invoking, as in the past
they might have the Garden or the Palace, that which
was not yet stolen nor ruin: THE POEM.

LILY

Across dusk's pomegranate-strewn courtyard
the door to Lily's lighted room is open.

Earlier, she'd taken me to the touristic police station
to register my presence. When I'd signed my name,

she and the trinity of young officers stared at my script,
humoured: *decomposing, formless, a bad character.*

Isn't that my metaphysics, of granite statues fragmented,
heroes nameless, faces like God's, evasive, shimmering on the Deep?

Whereas Lily, mentored by the three-thousand year old junipers
of the Tibetan Plateau, studying tree rings, ancient weather

at the edge of geological time, might have another,
of Reoccurrence, in her love of Nature and opera –

    Her empty room is filled with Voice!

Though she's not there I can still see her under a high-altitude sky,
staring down at a miniscule flower, beholden by its signature.

MORNINGS

Hooked on a clothes line seven storeys up,
behind a rusted apartment building,

every balcony either glassed-in or barred,
there, each morning, is hung a small square cage.

Captive in this taunt against the sky,
in that reflective gap between call or song,

that Void birds have 'gifted' us,
there in the fixed perversity of a vertigo,

the finch is flapping sporadically, disarmed,
mute. No, manically vocal, but unheard.

We want this to be an ode.

"ICH BIN CHINESE"

Being existent
was for Kafka
what my name
is:

IN THE MUSEUM

(Moist white paper, primordial, covers the inscribed,
be that a bronze vessel, rock or cliff-face.
Then comes the hand, godly, breath across the water,
tamping the paper over the surface, experience
pressing things into matter, wrinkles into a blank face.
Again: the hand. This time with a ball of material,
a thundercloud, maybe, that's thumped against an inkpad,
then against the white, thumped with the rhythm
of massage, a defibrillation to awaken an image
or even an Arabic word, to evoke, through the mists
of ink, paper's epidermal openness, until,
with both hands, the grafted – now dry – is lifted away, kite-light.)

Daily, a man is employed by this in the Museum of Steles.

"CHEMIN DE L'ÂME"

When, as in a mirror, the words
engraved on the stele are backward,
we, the Dead, inside the rock, captured,
read every word, echoing what's heard.

LESSON ON ALLUSION

"… wind you cannot read
so why do you turn the pages?"

The Qing Emperor sentenced
the poet to death
for that ' ',
for what he heard
was singular,
his Name, a breeze
speaking through
allusion's empty
mirror.

YINYUAN LONGQI *AKA* INGEN RYUKI

– recalling his ink-brush painting in the National Gallery, Melbourne

Although this doesn't translate,
in the Temple of Mind
a monk,
having abandoned the quest
for his vanished father,
taken the Dharma and tea
to Nagasaki, then Uji,
that old man, writing,
remembers encountering
Kuan-yin
face-to-face:

    MOUNTAIN BRIGHT, LIKE SNOW

THE COUPLE

There, in the half-empty restaurant,
you are watching the young couple,
how they are talking; he is subtle,
trying to explain himself. You, too,
'have been there'. When the little tears
escape her, trail down her face, untouched,
frozen in what the words belittle,
that interruption, blank, the 'breaking-up',
only varying in intensity, not name,
you see her brittle presence,
our every hope, as just another ruin.

EXILE

– after Bei Dao

I am the roaming wind, you are the fossil …

GHOST WEDDING

– for Hoe Fang

The boy was playing in his parents' room,
creeping under their bed in that first game
of disappearance. He found the shrine
his mother hid there: oranges, joss sticks, a photo.
He asked:

    "Who is in that picture, that little girl?"

"Your sister. She died before you were born."

He was happy in newly revealed siblinghood, his playmate,
deep in the familiar Unknown, a ghost.

~

Over the years his mother worried for her daughter's
happiness. She hired a matchmaker to seek
someone suitable, someone who had also died young,
who could be a good ghost-husband. He was found
across the border, on the Mainland, that side
of the Chinese Mirror. Eventually they were married,
making both the mothers happy.

~

Then years later, when he and his mother
were visiting their clan village, where
they found out that his father had for decades
been funding the local schools and were treated
like celebrities, they realized the ghost son-in-law's
village was near. His mother declared:

"We must visit our relatives."

~

> Not a village: high-rises over smoke
> and rubble, like Tang Dynasty mountains!

~

His mother rheumatoid, pained, looked up
at the five flights of stairs between her and family.
He asked her if that might be too much.

"No. We must pay our respects."

Then began her ascent in his arms,
her own, toughly sensitive, encircling his neck,
the two of them, frail mother and devoted son,
lightened, almost pushed up the stairs
by ghostly hands.

AMONG THE MUSLIMS

      Two ghosts wandering, lost,
through Xian's Muslim Quarter.
      One believes he was Kafir,
last seen in the Portuguese Empire.
      The other, 'malay', dreams
he's in Bo-Kaap or Cairo,
      somewhere in Africa.
They converse, not like angels,
      more like reborn
son and eternal father.
      They're sure there's no-one
other than Allah to eavesdrop
here.

THE POET

We won't find The Poet
in his words. That's why
we visit their houses
or their graves, or rivers.
There's no space in a poem
for The Poet, only the said
and, sometimes, memories.
We visit the countries of foreign
poets to find them ruined,
to witness, where once words
were, rubble, beheaded statues
and birds, caged songbirds.

THE DREAMS

"Gweilo," he crooned. "Gweilo."
We were both drunk. The taxidriver, too.
We'd spent all day on translations, then
went roaming the Foreigners' District.
He gestured through the window to Tiananmen
Square: "Hakgwei! You expected what?"
From the Forbidden City's gate a postage-stamp Mao
flew past us and into the rear-view mirror.
I didn't answer, was nodding off, could hear him
singing in the empty taxi of my skull.
We were in Africa, arms and torsos against
the windows, the car trembling with the passing mob.
Couldn't tell who they were or if they upheld
small red books or wooden AK-47s
or Europeans ideas like pasteis de nata.
Then they were rocking the taxi. No, I was waking.
My translator, an albino anaconda
uncurling over me across the backseat,
hissed with vodka's forked tongue, his voice
in my ear only. Under my breath I started
my own mantra, like when in the mirror
the Devil's face had been mine
and I'd chanted forcefully, loud and fast,
from deep within my belly where Tsafendas
had said his sleeping snake was. Mine is here,
asking, "Where are you going now?"
I want to say, *Back into the Dream of Revolution,*
but don't want to be that museum curator
beaten by peasants till mute. He's pointing
at a cenotaph: "One of those steles that obsess you;

Monument to the People's Heroes. At its face
Mao signed-on, as you say, wrote …"
My eyes are closing again. Another tiny Mao, silent,
accelerated by my mantra, is speeding closer.
Are we circling a massive stupa?
In the flickering dimness, tumbling into a canyon,
I am that boy running across the dark Chengdu intersection,
a blur, small thuds, screech of the stopping black car.
I'd run forward, and a woman, too. Too late – he'd risen,
was running, sprinting into the purified night.
Awake now. My translator is humming a tune,
possibly from his youth, something sentimental
– "The East is Red"? – and his eyes
are closed, or appear to be.

TO SEGALEN

Let Name be between voice and face.

Let Name be the void
between the speaking Dead
and that impossible Han portrait
sought in the China of Self.

Don't be found there under that squat stone horse,
barbaric, trapped in the rictus that is likeness,
a cipher printed by an army tank.

Don't –

THE KISS
– for M

That kiss, a Sichuan peppery aftertaste,
minty, is moonlight whispered then sung,
even when she has gone eight thousand miles away
and is remembered first by my languorous tongue.

THE DEMON

Ever since reading
that the house of
the Chief of the Secret Police
was not far from mine,
north of the Drum and Bell Towers
that regulated pre-modern
thought in this capital,
I've been praying to rid myself
of the idea that Avalokitesvara
has a doppelgänger,
an 'evil twin';
the image of him
a functionary, torturer,
schizophrenic
typical of Empire …
that demonic
calligrapher, ambidextrous,
timeless, personifying
the Mirror,
its profanity.

THAT POEM

This poem, copied by another poet,
begins in that language said not to be sound
and becomes, on first reflection, meaning,
then, when aloud, twinned, pure noise.
And again, its errant music, a phantasia,
is all we have here on the far side
of our senses, where we are nameless,
faceless, imageless, the completion
of who we were to be to others
in their caves, or in our Manifestation.

LANDSCAPIST

– for Mu Xin, the painter

Unroll the miniature scroll
  that someone long ago
would have kept
  up their sleeve
in case of boredom. Let's
  see what the brush
of the landscapist
  has given us
instead of our vernacular
  blindness. This
quick and unblinking
  valley of steep cliffs,
river blankly rushing into Name,
  this, our looking,
despite ourselves, is
  a quietude and an effacement,
a turning to the imaginary
  wall to see, further,
above the overlapping long ridges
  rising from haze,
cloud or broad flash of river,
  a dark bronze pagoda.
And you are there, tiny,
  hand shading your eyes,
staring back at us against
  the swaths of brightness,
over the vast pure ache
  of distance, amber
river, sudden rocks

and small mountains,
their decalcomania,
        shadows, that were
the Abyss and are now
        smudged surface.

~

Your hand, dear Reader,
        wants to pass over
this picture, this mirror,
        but can't.
It is a wall untouchable,
        recently painted. Besides,
you don't exist.

ACKNOWLEDGEMENTS

The poems in this volume have appeared in various publications before, often being reprinted in later books and sometimes in anthologies. The works' initial publication were:

Mister! Mister! Mister! (Medan: Australia Centre Medan, 1999)

The Ancient Capital of Images, with Japanese translation by Keiji Minato (Kyoto: privately published)

The poems of "Singapore and the Real" appeared in *Over There: Poems from Australia and Singapore* (Singapore: Ethos Books, 2008)

This Dark Book, with Portuguese translation by Inês Dias (Lisbon: Averno, 2012)

The above suites of poems also were reprinted, with some changes, in the following collections:

Loanwords (Fremantle: Fremantle Arts Centre Press, 2002)

The Ancient Capital of Images (Fremantle: FACP, 2005)

Elsewhere (Cambridge: Salt Publishing, 2007)

The author would like to acknowledge all those individuals and institutions who over the years during which he wrote these poems provided financial support and various kinds of stimulation. And he especially thanks, as always, his translators and friends.

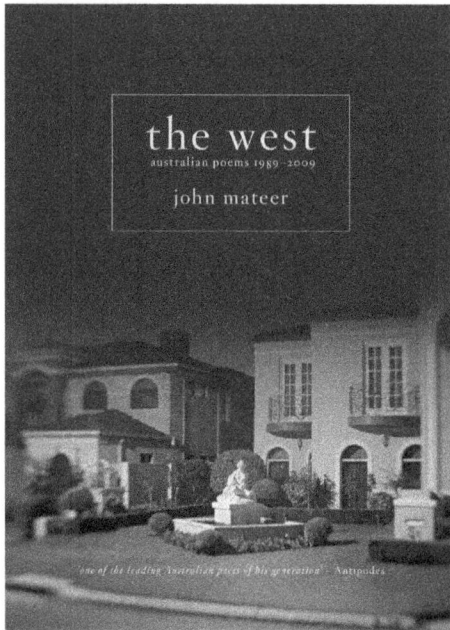

the west
australian poems 1989–2009

john mateer

'one of the leading Australian poets of his generation' Antipodes

Antipodes has described Mateer's work as 'risky and experimental' while the *Australian Book Review* has noted his 'force and directness'. *The Weekend Australian* has said that Mateer is a poet 'brilliantly and very differently writing himself into this country'.

A timely and rewarding retrospective, *The West: Australian Poems 1989–2009* represents twenty years of work by internationally renowned poet John Mateer. Taking its bearings from the Indian Ocean, Mateer's poetry crisscrosses the continent, inviting the reader on a journey into the psyche, culture and landscape of this country.

With an introduction by Martin Harrison.

ISBN 9781921361869

www.ingramcontent.com/pod-product-compliance
Lightning Source LLC
Chambersburg PA
CBHW021148090426
42740CB00008B/998